Half Baked Harvest Cookbook:60+ Healthy Recipe,Simple and Delicious Food

BY

Samuel Vega

3

Contents

1.Half and Halfs

<u>Ingredients</u>

- 1 ½ cups all-purpose flour
- ¼ teaspoon baking soda
- 1 pinch salt
- ½ cup butter, softened
- ¼ cup white sugar
- ½ cup brown sugar
- 1 egg
- 1 teaspoon vanilla extract
- 1 cup milk chocolate chips
- 1 ½ cups all-purpose flour
- ¼ teaspoon baking soda
- salt
- ¼ cup unsweetened cocoa powder
- ½ cup butter, softened
- ½ cup brown sugar
- ½ cup white sugar
- 1 egg

- 1 teaspoon vanilla extract
- 1 cup milk chocolate chips

Headings

- Stage 1
- Preheat the broiler to 300 degrees F (150 degrees C).
- Stage 2
- In a medium bowl, cream together 1/2 cup margarine with 1/4 cup white sugar and 1/2 cup earthy colored sugar. Beat in 1 egg and 1 teaspoon vanilla. Consolidate 1/2 cups flour with 1/4 teaspoon of heating pop and a spot of salt, mix into the creamed combination until all around mixed. Overlay in the chocolate chips.
- Stage 3
- In another medium bowl, cream together 1/2 cup margarine with 1/2 cup white sugar and 1/2 cup earthy colored sugar. Beat in 1 egg and 1 teaspoon vanilla. Consolidate 1/2 cups flour with 1/4 cup cocoa, 1/4 teaspoon of heating pop and a spot of salt, mix into the creamed combination until all around mixed. Overlay in the chocolate chips. Scoop a limited quantity of every mixture onto an enormous spoon, drop treats 2 inches separated onto an ill-equipped treat sheet.
- Stage 4
- Prepare for 8 to 10 minutes in the preheated broiler. Permit treats to cool on preparing sheet for 5 minutes prior to eliminating to a wire rack to cool totally.

2.Half and Half Cocktail

Ingredients

- 8 fluid ounces pale ale
- 8 fluid ounces stout

Bearings

- Stage 1
- Fill 1/2 a 16 ounces glass with pale beer. Gradually fill the rest of the glass with strong, pouring it gradually over the rear of a spoon to layer it on top.

3.Patsy's Half-Baked Blueberry Pie

Ingredients

- 1 refrigerated crust for a 9-inch pie
- ½ (8 ounce) package cream cheese
- 2 ½ cups fresh blueberries
- 3 tablespoons cornstarch
- 1 cup cold water
- 2 ½ cups fresh blueberries
- 1 cup white sugar
- 1 pinch lemon zest

Bearings

- Stage 1
- Preheat stove to 350 degrees F (175 degrees C).
- Stage 2
- Press pie outside mixture into a pie dish. Punch little holes into batter with a fork.

- Stage 3
- Prepare in the preheated broiler until delicately carmelized, around 15 minutes. Cool to room temperature.
- Stage 4
- Spot cream cheddar in a little microwave-safe bowl; heat in microwave on High to mellow, around 20 seconds.
- Stage 5
- Spread mellowed cream cheddar in the lower part of cooled covering.
- Stage 6
- Layer 2 1/2 cups blueberries over the cream cheddar.
- Stage 7
- Whisk cornstarch and cold water in a little bowl until broke down.
- Stage 8
- Mix cornstarch blend, 2 1/2 cups blueberries, sugar, and lemon zing in a pan over medium warmth; stew until thickened, 5 to 10 minutes.
- Stage 9
- Pour the thickened blueberry blend over the crude blueberries in the pie covering and spread equally.
- Stage 10
- Cool pie in cooler until set, somewhere around 60 minutes.

4.Creamy Shrimp Scampi with Half-and-Half

Ingredients

- ½ (16 ounce) package linguine pasta
- 4 tablespoons butter
- 2 cloves garlic, minced
- 1 pound jumbo shrimp, peeled and deveined
- 2 tablespoons Pinot Grigio wine
- 2 teaspoons lemon juice, or to taste
- ½ cup half-and-half
- ¼ cup finely shredded Parmesan cheese
- 2 tablespoons chopped fresh parsley, or to taste

Headings

- Stage 1

- Heat an enormous pot of softly salted water to the point of boiling. Cook linguine at a bubble until delicate yet firm to the nibble, around 8 minutes.
- Stage 2
- While pasta cooks, liquefy 2 tablespoons margarine in a skillet over medium warmth. Add garlic and cook until fragrant and daintily seared, around 1 moment. Add shrimp and cook until tails begin twisting in, around 2 minutes for each side. Add remaining spread, Pinot Grigio, lemon juice, cream, and Parmesan cheddar. Mix to join.
- Stage 3
- Channel linguine and split noodles between 2 dishes. Serve shrimp combination on top and embellishment with parsley.

5.Fall Harvest Baked Apples

Ingredients

- 8 red apples, cored
- ¼ cup butter
- ⅓ cup maple syrup
- ½ teaspoon ground cinnamon
- ⅓ teaspoon ground ginger
- ½ lemon, juiced
- 1 teaspoon vanilla extract
- ⅓ cup coarsely chopped walnuts (Optional)

Bearings

- Stage 1
- Preheat stove to 350 degrees F (175 degrees C). Spot apples in a 9x13 inch preparing dish.
- Stage 2
- In a little pot over medium warmth, consolidate margarine, maple syrup, cinnamon, ginger, lemon juice and vanilla. Heat to the point of boiling, and sprinkle similarly over apples.
- Stage 3
- Cover with foil, and prepare in preheated broiler for 20 minutes. Eliminate cover, and keep on preparing for 10 minutes, or until apples are delicate. Serve warm.

6.Harvest Slaw

Ingredients

- ¼ cup chopped pecans
- 1 (8.5 ounce) package coleslaw mix
- ½ cup matchstick-style shredded carrots
- 1 ½ cups red grapes
- ¼ cup crumbled feta cheese
- ½ cup mayonnaise
- ½ cup Ranch dressing
- 1 tablespoon sugar

Bearings

- Stage 1
- In a medium ungreased skillet, over medium warmth, toast the walnuts by mixing habitually until brilliant brown. Put away to cool.
- Stage 2
- In a huge bowl, consolidate coleslaw blend, carrots, grapes, walnuts, and feta cheddar.

- Stage 3
- In a little bowl, mix together the mayonnaise, and Ranch dressing. Pour in sugar, and blend until broke down. Throw coleslaw combination with dressing until uniformly covered. Serve quickly, or cover and chill in fridge.

7.Harvest Salad

Ingredients

- ½ cup chopped walnuts
- 1 bunch spinach, rinsed and torn into bite-size pieces
- ½ cup dried cranberries
- ½ cup crumbled blue cheese
- 2 tomatoes, chopped
- 1 avocado - peeled, pitted and diced
- ½ red onion, thinly sliced

- 2 tablespoons red raspberry jam (with seeds)
- 2 tablespoons red wine vinegar
- ⅓ cup walnut oil
- freshly ground black pepper to taste
- salt to taste

Bearings

- Stage 1
- Preheat stove to 375 degrees F (190 degrees C). Organize pecans in a solitary layer on a heating sheet. Toast in stove for 5 minutes, or until nuts start to brown.
- Stage 2
- In a huge bowl, throw together the spinach, pecans, cranberries, blue cheddar, tomatoes, avocado, and red onion.
- Stage 3
- In a little bowl, whisk together jam, vinegar, pecan oil, pepper, and salt. Pour over the plate of mixed greens not long prior to serving, and throw to cover.

8.Harvest Pasta Bake

<u>Ingredients</u>

- 1 (2 pound) butternut squash, peeled, cut into 1-inch cubes
- 1 onion, cut lengthwise in half, then sliced crosswise
- ½ teaspoon crushed red pepper
- 2 tablespoons olive oil
- 3 ⅓ cups rigatoni pasta, uncooked
- 4 ounces PHILADELPHIA Cream Cheese, cubed, softened
- ¼ cup milk
- 1 (8 ounce) package KRAFT Shredded Three Cheese with a TOUCH OF PHILADELPHIA, divided
- ¼ cup croutons, crushed

<u>Bearings</u>

- Stage 1
- Warmth stove to 400 degrees F.
- Stage 2
- Consolidate initial 4 fixings in 13x9-inch heating dish. Heat 30 to 40 min. or then again until squash is delicate. In the mean time, cook pasta as coordinated on bundle, precluding salt.
- Stage 3
- Channel pasta; return to container. Add cream cheddar and milk; mix until cream cheddar is softened and sauce is very much mixed. Add to crush combination with 1 cup destroyed cheddar; blend gently. Top with bread garnish morsels and staying destroyed cheddar.
- Stage 4
- Heat 20 min. or then again until warmed through.

9.Chocolate-Glazed Mochi Doughnuts

Ingredients

- 2 cups sweet rice flour (mochiko), divided
- 3 tablespoons milk
- ½ cup milk
- 1 egg
- ¼ cup granulated sugar
- 1 ½ teaspoons baking powder
- 3 tablespoons unsalted butter, melted
- 1 teaspoon vanilla
- Reynolds® Parchment Paper
- Vanilla Glaze (optional):
- 2 cups powdered sugar
- 6 tablespoons unsalted butter, melted
- 1 teaspoon vanilla
- 5 tablespoons warm water, or as needed

- Chocolate Glaze:
- ⅓ cup coconut milk
- 12 ounces dark chocolate, chopped
- ⅓ cup powdered sugar
- Flaky sea salt, for topping

Bearings

- Stage 1
- In a microwave-safe bowl, whisk together 1/4 cup sweet rice flour and 3 tablespoons milk. Microwave on high for 30 seconds, mix and afterward cook one more 20 to 30 seconds longer or until the batter is cooked through, looks obscure and is fun, yet not really cooked that it is dry. The combination should in any case be wet. Put away to cool marginally.
- Stage 2
- In the bowl of a stand blender with the mixture snare connected (you can likewise do this the hard way, however a stand blender makes it a lot simpler), add the excess 1 3/4 cups sweet rice flour, 1/2 cup milk, egg, granulated sugar, heating powder, margarine and vanilla. Add the cooled, cooked rice flour combination.
- Stage 3
- Ply the batter on low speed until the mixture meets up. Speed up to medium and ply until the blend is totally smooth and blended, around 3 to 5 minutes. The mixture will be tacky.
- Stage 4

- Line a heating sheet with Reynolds® Parchment Paper.
- Stage 5
- Sprinkle a spotless surface with rice flour and scratch the mixture out onto the floured surface. Sprinkle the mixture with enough flour to keep it from staying. Carry the batter out until is it 1/2 inch thick. Remove however many doughnuts as you can, utilizing a 3-inch bread roll shaper for the doughnuts and a 1-inch roll shaper for the donut openings. Spot the doughnuts on the pre-arranged preparing sheet as you work. Accumulate any pieces of mixture back into a ball and carry the batter out. Cut however many doughnuts as you can and rehash the cycle, you ought to get around 10 doughnuts.
- Stage 6
- In a substantial lined pot, heat 3 to 4 crawls of oil to 330 degrees F. Try not to release the oil more than 350 degrees F - or the donut will consume before the inner parts are completely cooked. Fry the doughnuts in clusters for 2 to 3 minutes for every side. Channel onto a paper towel lined heating plate. Rehash until every one of the doughnuts have been singed. Permit to cool somewhat prior to coating.
- Stage 7
- In the event that plunging the doughnuts in the vanilla frosting first, do as such now and let them dry on a cooling rack for 5 minutes prior to dunking in the chocolate glaze.

- Stage 8
- Vanilla Glaze (discretionary): In a bowl, whisk together the powdered sugar, margarine and vanilla. Add water, 1 tablespoon at a time, until the coating has arrived at your ideal consistency. Dunk every donut in the frost and permit any overabundance to dribble off. Spot the donut on a cooling rack and rehash with the excess doughnuts.
- Stage 9
- Chocolate Glaze: Place the cream in a little sauce dish and bring to a stew. Eliminate from the warmth and mix in the chocolate until liquefied and smooth. Add the powdered sugar and vanilla, mixing until smooth. Let cool somewhat.
- Stage 10
- Plunge or sprinkle every donut with the frosting. Sprinkle with flaky ocean salt. Eat.

10.Vanilla Half-Moons

Ingredients

- ¾ cup butter, softened
- ½ cup white sugar
- 2 egg yolks
- 1 ½ vanilla beans, divided
- 1 ½ cups all-purpose flour
- ½ cup ground almonds
- 2 cups confectioners' sugar for rolling

Headings

- Stage 1
- In a medium bowl, cream together the margarine and white sugar until smooth. Beat in the egg yolks each in turn. Split the portion of vanilla bean and scratch the seeds; mix the seeds into the margarine blend. Blend in the flour and ground almonds. Gap the batter into two pieces, wrap and refrigerate until firm.
- Stage 2
- Preheat broiler to 350 degrees F (175 degrees C). Line treat sheets with material paper. Sever tablespoonful measured bits of batter and roll them into little ropes around 2 inches long. Curve the ropes into a half circle and spot them 2 inches separated onto the pre-arranged treat sheets.
- Stage 3
- Heat for 10 to 15 minutes in the preheated stove, until softly seared. Scratch the seeds from the excess vanilla bean and mix them into

the confectioners' sugar. Cautiously roll warm treats in the vanilla sugar.

11.Harvest Yams

Ingredients

- 3 large yams, quartered length-wise
- ¾ cup maple syrup
- 1 teaspoon ground nutmeg
- 1 ½ teaspoons ground cinnamon
- ½ cup butter, sliced

Headings

- Stage 1
- Preheat broiler to 325 degrees F (165 degrees C).
- Stage 2
- Lay sweet potatoes skin side down in a 9x12 inch heating dish. Pour maple syrup over the sweet potatoes and sprinkle with nutmeg and

cinnamon. Dab with spread and cover with aluminum foil.

- Stage 3
- Heat in preheated stove for 25 minutes.

12.Half-Red Half-Sweet Potato Salad

<u>Ingredients</u>

- 3 pounds red potatoes
- 2 ½ pounds sweet potatoes
- ¼ cup white wine vinegar
- ¼ cup olive oil
- 1 clove garlic, minced
- ¼ cup dill pickle relish
- ½ cup chopped red onion
- ⅓ cup mayonnaise
- 1 pinch ground black pepper
- ⅓ cup sour cream
- ½ cup chopped parsley

Headings

- Stage 1
- Heat an enormous pot of salted water to the point of boiling. Add potatoes; cook until delicate yet at the same time firm, around 15 minutes. Channel, cool and cut.
- Stage 2
- In an enormous bowl, join the vinegar, olive oil, garlic, dill pickle relish and onion. Blend and cover with cut potatoes.
- Stage 3
- Whisk together mayonnaise, pepper, harsh cream and parsley. Pour over potatoes and chill somewhere around 8 hours.

13.Harvest Vegetable Bread

Ingredients

- 1 cup mashed potatoes
- ¾ cup Almond Breeze Original Unsweetened almondmilk
- ⅓ cup vegetable oil
- 1 egg
- ¾ cup shredded zucchini
- ⅓ cup minced sun-dried tomato (preferably smoked)
- ⅓ cup sliced green onion tops
- 3 ½ cups flour, plus extra for kneading
- 1 ½ tablespoons baking powder
- ½ teaspoon salt
- ½ cup shredded parmesan cheese

Bearings

- Stage 1
- Preheat stove to 375 degrees F and line a heating sheet with material paper or daintily oil.
- Stage 2
- Mix together pureed potatoes, Almond Breeze, oil, and egg in a huge bowl until very much blended. Mix in zucchini, sun-dried tomatoes, and green onions. Mix together excess fixings in a medium bowl and mix into vegetable blend.
- Stage 3
- Move to a floured load up and work a few times until mixture is smooth (don't add a lot of flour or bread will be intense). Shape into a portion and spot on pre-arranged preparing sheet.

- Stage 4
- Prepare for 55 minutes or until a toothpick embedded into the middle confesses all.

14. Harvest Pepper and Chicken Pasta

Ingredients

- 1 (16 ounce) package bow-tie pasta
- olive oil
- 2 chicken breasts, cut into thin strips
- 1 onion, diced
- 1 orange bell pepper, diced
- 1 red bell pepper, diced
- 1 clove garlic, minced, or more to taste
- 1 teaspoon dried basil
- ½ teaspoon red pepper flakes
- ½ (26 ounce) jar tomato sauce (such as Newman's Own®)

Bearings

- Stage 1
- Heat a huge pot of daintily salted water to the point of boiling. Cook necktie pasta at a bubble, mixing sporadically, until delicate yet firm to the nibble, around 12 minutes. Channel.
- Stage 2
- Warmth oil in a skillet over medium-high warmth. Add chicken tenders; cook and mix until as of now not pink in the middle and the juices run clear, 5 to 7 minutes. Move to a plate fixed with paper towels.
- Stage 3
- Decrease heat under skillet to medium; add onion, orange chime pepper, red ringer pepper, garlic, dried basil, and red pepper drops to skillet. Cook and mix until onions are clear and peppers are mellowed, 3 to 5 minutes. Add pureed tomatoes; heat for around 2 minutes. Add chicken; cook for one more 2 to 3 minutes. Piece cooked pasta into bowls; spoon chicken and sauce combination on top.

15.Tito's Harvest Punch

Ingredients

- 8 ounces Tito's Handmade Vodka
- 1 (750 milliliter) bottle Prosecco
- 1 gallon apple cider
- 24 ounces ginger beer
- 3 apples, sliced
- 2 oranges, sliced into triangles
- 8 cinnamon sticks
- Cinnamon sugar, for rimming glasses

Bearings

- Stage 1
- Add all fixings to a huge punch bowl.
- Stage 2
- Give the punch a mix and present with cinnamon sugar-rimmed glasses. Allow your visitors to add their own ice, so the punch doesn't become watered down.

16.Grenadine Half-Mast

Ingredients

- 1 cup ice
- 6 fluid ounces sweet and sour mix
- 3 fluid ounces tequila
- 1 ½ fluid ounces grenadine syrup
- 1 fluid ounce triple sec (orange-flavored liqueur)

Bearings

- Stage 1
- Fill a huge glass with ice. Pour prepared blend, tequila, grenadine, and triple sec over the ice; mix.

17.Harvest Pumpkin Cupcakes

Ingredients

- Cupcakes:
- 4 eggs, slightly beaten
- ¾ cup Mazola® Vegetable Plus! Oil
- 2 cups sugar
- 1 (15 ounce) can pumpkin
- 1 ¾ cups all-purpose flour
- ¼ cup Argo® OR Kingsford's® Corn Starch
- 4 teaspoons Spice Islands® Pumpkin Pie Spice
- 2 teaspoons Argo® Baking Powder
- 1 teaspoon baking soda
- ¾ teaspoon salt
- Frosting:
- 1 (8 ounce) package cream cheese, softened
- 3 tablespoons butter OR margarine, softened
- 1 tablespoon orange juice

- 2 teaspoons Spice Islands® 100% Pure Bourbon Vanilla Extract
- 1 ½ teaspoons freshly grated orange peel
- 4 cups powdered sugar

<u>Headings</u>

- Stage 1
- To make cupcakes: Blend the eggs, oil, sugar, and pumpkin in an enormous blending bowl; put away. Mix together dry fixings in a different bowl. Add dry fixings to pumpkin combination and beat until all around mixed. Fill lined biscuit tins. Fill around 2/3 full. Prepare in preheated 350 degrees stove for 30 minutes or until focus springs back when contacted. Cool 30 minutes. Spread with icing.
- Stage 2
- To make icing: Beat cream cheddar and margarine until fleecy. Add remaining fixings and beat until smooth. Spread over cooled cupcakes.

18.Harvest Walnut Pumpkin Pie

__Ingredients__

- 1 (15 ounce) can plain pumpkin puree
- 1 (14 ounce) can sweetened condensed milk
- 2 eggs
- 1 teaspoon maple-flavored extract
- ½ teaspoon ground cinnamon
- ½ teaspoon salt
- ¼ teaspoon ground ginger
- ¼ teaspoon ground nutmeg
- 1 (9 inch) prepared graham cracker crust
- Walnut Topping:
- ⅓ cup packed brown sugar
- ⅓ cup all-purpose flour
- ½ teaspoon ground cinnamon
- 3 tablespoons butter, cubed
- ½ cup chopped walnuts

Bearings

- Stage 1
- Preheat the stove to 425 degrees F (220 degrees C).
- Stage 2
- Consolidate pumpkin, dense milk, eggs, maple extricate, cinnamon, salt, ginger, and nutmeg in a huge bowl. Blend well and fill the graham wafer outside. Smooth the top with a spatula.
- Stage 3
- Prepare in the preheated stove for 15 minutes. Decrease stove temperature to 350 degrees F (175 degrees C). Keep preparing until filling is set, around 30 minutes.
- Stage 4
- Get ready pecan besting while pie is preparing. Blend earthy colored sugar, flour, and cinnamon together in a bowl. Cut in spread with a fork until coarse scraps structure. Mix in pecans.
- Stage 5
- Eliminate pie from the stove and cover equally with the fixing. Keep preparing until garnish is brilliant brown, around 10 minutes. Cool totally prior to cutting.

19.Harvest Rice Dish

Ingredients

- ½ cup slivered almonds
- 2 cups chicken broth
- ½ cup uncooked brown rice
- ½ cup uncooked wild rice
- 3 tablespoons butter
- 3 onions, sliced into 1/2 inch wedges
- 1 tablespoon brown sugar
- 1 cup dried cranberries
- ⅔ cup fresh sliced mushrooms
- ½ teaspoon orange zest
- salt and pepper to taste

Headings

- Stage 1

- Spot almonds on an ungreased heating sheet. Toast at 350 degrees F (175 degrees C) for 5 to 8 minutes.
- Stage 2
- Blend stock, earthy colored rice, and wild rice in a medium pan, and bring to bubble. Lessen warmth to low, cover, and stew 45 minutes, until rice is delicate and stock is assimilated.
- Stage 3
- In medium skillet, soften spread over medium-high warmth. Add onions and earthy colored sugar. Saute until margarine is assimilated and onions are clear and delicate. Lessen warmth, and cook onions for an additional 20 minutes, until they are caramelized.
- Stage 4
- Mix cranberries and mushrooms into the skillet. Cover, and cook 10 minutes or until berries begin to expand. Mix in almonds and orange zing, then, at that point, overlap the blend into the cooked rice. Salt and pepper to taste.

20.Harvest Pasta Bake with PHILADELPHIA Cooking Creme

<u>Ingredients</u>

- 1 (2 pound) butternut squash, peeled and cut into 1-inch cubes
- 1 red onion, cut into 1 inch pieces
- ¼ teaspoon crushed red pepper
- 2 tablespoons olive oil
- 4 cups rigatoni pasta, uncooked
- 1 (10 ounce) tub Philadelphia Italian Three Cheese Cooking Creme
- 2 cups KRAFT 4 Cheese Italiano Shredded Cheese, divided

<u>Headings</u>

- Stage 1
- Warmth broiler to 400 degrees F.
- Stage 2

- Join initial 4 fixings in 13x9-inch preparing dish showered with cooking splash.
- Stage 3
- Heat 30 to 40 min. or then again until squash is delicate. In the mean time, cook pasta as coordinated on bundle, excluding salt.
- Stage 4
- Channel pasta, holding 1/3 cup cooking water. Add to crush combination with Cooking Creme, saved water and 1 cup destroyed cheddar; blend gently. Top with staying destroyed cheddar.
- Stage 5
- Heat 20 min. or then again until warmed through.

21.Healthy Harvest Soup

Ingredients

- 2 tablespoons vegetable oil
- 1 onion, chopped
- 1 tablespoon chopped garlic
- 1 teaspoon dried sage
- 1 teaspoon dried thyme
- 8 cups vegetable broth
- 2 acorn squash - peeled, seeded, and chopped
- 2 cups water
- 1 (15 ounce) can kidney beans, rinsed and drained
- ½ cup quinoa
- ½ cup pot barley
- ½ teaspoon salt
- 1 bunch kale, stemmed and coarsely chopped

Headings

- Stage 1
- Warmth vegetable oil in an enormous pot over medium-high warmth; saute onion in hot oil until relaxed and somewhat brilliant, 5 to 10 minutes. Add garlic; saute until brilliant and fragrant, 2 to 4 minutes more. Mix sage and thyme in onion blend and saute until fragrant, around 30 seconds.
- Stage 2
- Mix vegetable stock, squash, water, kidney beans, quinoa, grain, and salt into onion combination; heat to the point of boiling, lessen warmth to medium-low, and stew until grain is delicate and soup flavors consolidate, around 35 minutes.
- Stage 3

- Mix kale into soup; stew until kale is delicate, around 10 minutes.

22.Autumn Harvest Cookies

<u>Ingredients</u>

- 1 cup softened butter
- ½ cup brown sugar
- ½ cup white sugar
- 2 eggs
- ½ teaspoon orange extract
- ½ teaspoon vanilla extract
- 1 ½ cups all-purpose flour
- ¼ teaspoon salt
- 1 teaspoon baking powder
- 1 teaspoon pumpkin pie spice
- 2 ½ cups rolled oats
- ½ cup chopped walnuts
- 1 cup dried cranberries

<u>Headings</u>

- Stage 1

- Preheat broiler to 350 degrees F (175 degrees C). Line a heating sheet with material paper.
- Stage 2
- Cream together margarine and the brown and white sugars in a bowl until smooth. Beat in the eggs, vanilla and orange concentrate.
- Stage 3
- In a different bowl, join the flour, salt, heating powder and pumpkin pie flavor; mix flour blend into the sugar combination. Add the moved oats, pecans and cranberries and blend completely. Utilizing a little frozen yogurt scoop or teaspoon, drop adjusted scoops of mixture onto the pre-arranged treat sheet.
- Stage 4
- Heat in the preheated broiler until the edges are brilliant, 8 to 10 minutes. Permit the treats to cool on the preparing sheet for 1 moment prior to eliminating to a wire rack to cool totally.

23.Harvest Potato Soup

Ingredients

- 2 tablespoons butter
- 2 onions, chopped
- 2 carrots, diced
- 1 stalk celery, diced
- 2 cloves garlic, minced
- 1 cup cauliflower florets
- 1 cup diced zucchini
- 6 large potatoes, cubed
- 3 cups vegetable broth
- 1 cup chopped kale, or to taste
- ¼ cup evaporated milk
- 1 bay leaf
- ½ cup corn kernels
- 1 teaspoon smoked paprika
- 1 teaspoon chopped fresh dill
- salt and ground black pepper to taste
- ½ cup shredded Cheddar cheese, or to taste (Optional)

- ½ cup chopped fresh parsley, or to taste (Optional)

Headings

- Stage 1
- Liquefy margarine in a stock pot over medium-low warmth. Cook and mix onions, carrots, celery, and garlic in hot margarine until the onions are clear, 5 to 10 minutes. Add cauliflower and zucchini to onion combination; cook until recently warmed, 1 to 2 minutes.
- Stage 2
- Mix potatoes and stock into vegetable combination; heat to the point of boiling. Diminish warmth and stew until potatoes are simply delicate, 15 to 20 minutes. Add kale to soup; cook until kale is somewhat shriveled, 2 to 3 minutes.
- Stage 3
- Empty milk into a blender and spoon around 2/3 the soup into blender, working in groups if necessary. Cover and hold top down; beat a couple of times prior to leaving on to mix until smooth, 1 to 2 minutes.
- Stage 4
- Empty pureed soup once more into stock pot; mix in corn, paprika, dill, salt, and pepper. Cook soup until corn is warmed, 2 to 3 minutes. Serve soup embellished with cheddar and parsley.

24.Harvest Pumpkin Dip

Ingredients

- 2 cups confectioners' sugar, sifted
- 1 (8 ounce) package cream cheese, softened
- 1 (15 ounce) can pumpkin
- 1 tablespoon pumpkin pie spice
- 1 teaspoon vanilla extract
- ½ teaspoon ground ginger

Headings

- Stage 1
- Mix confectioners' sugar and cream cheddar together in a bowl utilizing an electric blender. Add pumpkin, pumpkin pie zest, vanilla concentrate, and ground ginger; beat until smooth.

25.Harvest Noodle Pudding - Fruit Kugel

<u>Ingredients</u>

- 3 tablespoons butter, melted
- ½ (8 ounce) package wide egg noodles
- 1 large apple - peeled, cored, and chopped
- 1 large pear - peeled, cored, and chopped
- 1 tablespoon lemon juice
- 1 cup milk
- 4 eggs
- ½ cup applesauce
- ¼ cup white sugar
- 2 tablespoons light brown sugar
- 1 teaspoon vanilla extract
- ¼ teaspoon ground cinnamon
- ⅛ teaspoon salt
- 1 pinch ground nutmeg, or to taste
- ⅓ cup dried cranberries

Bearings

- Stage 1
- Preheat stove to 350 degrees F (175 degrees C).
- Stage 2
- Oil a 8x8-inch preparing dish with liquefied margarine.
- Stage 3
- Heat a huge pot of gently salted water to the point of boiling. Cook egg noodles in the bubbling water, mixing at times until cooked through however firm to the nibble, around 5 minutes. Channel.
- Stage 4
- Blend the apple and pear in with lemon juice in a bowl; put away.
- Stage 5
- Beat milk, eggs, fruit purée, white sugar, light earthy colored sugar, vanilla concentrate, cinnamon, salt, and nutmeg in an enormous bowl until recently consolidated.
- Stage 6
- Mix cranberries, egg noodles, and apple blend into the egg combination; pour in pre-arranged heating dish and cover preparing dish with aluminum foil.
- Stage 7
- Heat noodle pudding in preheated stove until set, 35 to 45 minutes.
- Stage 8

- Eliminate foil and return pudding to broiler to prepare until cooked, around 10 minutes more; cool to room temperature or serve chilled.

26.Harvest Tomato-Basil Rice with Pancetta

Ingredients

- 1 teaspoon olive oil
- ¼ pound pancetta bacon, diced
- 1 small onion, diced
- 1 zucchini, diced
- 1 (14.5 ounce) can no salt-added diced tomatoes, drained, juice reserved
- Water, as needed
- 1 (5.5 ounce) package Knorr® Rice Sides™ - Rice Pilaf
- 1 tablespoon chopped fresh basil

- 2 tablespoons grated Parmigiano-Reggiano cheese

Bearings

- Stage 1
- Warmth in a huge nonstick skillet over medium warmth. Add pancetta and onion and cook, mixing as often as possible, until the pancetta starts to deliver and the onions start to brown, around 4 minutes. Add the zucchini and cook until it starts to mellow, around 3 minutes. Mix in the depleted tomatoes and warmth through, around 1 moment. Move blend to a bowl.
- Stage 2
- Spot saved tomato juice is an estimating cup; add sufficient water to make 2 cups fluid.
- Stage 3
- In a similar skillet, add the tomato juice-water blend and heat to the point of boiling over high warmth. Mix in the Knorr® Rice Sides™ - Rice Pilaf. Lessen warmth to low and stew, covered, until rice is delicate, around 6 minutes.
- Stage 4
- Mix in pancetta, zucchini, onion, and tomato combination. Warmth through, 1 to 2 minutes. Sprinkle with basil and Parmigiano-Reggiano cheddar.

27.Winter Harvest Curry Stew

Ingredients

- 1 ½ gallons vegetable broth
- 4 butternut squashes - peeled, seeded, and diced
- 6 bunches mustard greens, chopped
- 7 heads cauliflower, cut into florets
- 7 heads broccoli, cut into florets
- 7 red bell peppers, diced
- 15 carrots, peeled and diced
- 15 parsnips, diced
- 1 ½ onions, diced
- 1 ½ stalks celery, diced
- ¾ cup raisins
- ¼ cup curry powder
- ¼ cup ground ginger
- ¼ cup ground cumin
- 1 ½ teaspoons cayenne pepper

Headings

- Stage 1
- Join vegetable stock, butternut squash, mustard greens, cauliflower, broccoli, red ringer peppers, carrots, parsnips, onions, celery, raisins, curry powder, ginger, cumin, and cayenne pepper in an enormous stockpot; heat to the point of boiling, decrease warmth to medium-low, and stew until the vegetables are delicate, around 60 minutes.

28.Harvest Loaf Cake

Ingredients

- 1 ¾ cups all-purpose flour
- 1 teaspoon baking soda
- 1 ½ teaspoons salt
- ¾ teaspoon ground nutmeg
- ½ teaspoon ground ginger
- ½ teaspoon ground cloves
- ½ cup butter

- 1 cup white sugar
- 2 eggs
- ¾ cup canned pumpkin
- ¾ cup semisweet chocolate chips
- ¾ cup chopped walnuts
- ¼ cup confectioners' sugar
- ¼ teaspoon ground nutmeg
- ¼ teaspoon ground cinnamon
- 2 tablespoons heavy cream

Bearings

- Stage 1
- Preheat stove to 350 degrees F (175 degrees C). Oil and flour a 9x5 inch portion container. In a medium bowl, blend flour, pop, salt, 3/4 teaspoon nutmeg, ginger and cloves. Put away.
- Stage 2
- In a huge bowl, cream spread and sugar until light and fleecy. Beat in the eggs. Add flour blend on the other hand with pumpkin. Mix in chocolate chips and 1/2 cup of the pecans. Empty hitter into portion container. Sprinkle staying nuts on top.
- Stage 3
- Prepare at 350 degrees F (175 degrees C) for 65 to 70 minutes or until toothpick embedded into focal point of cake tells the truth. While still warm, shower with coat. Cool for 6 hours prior to serving.
- Stage 4

- to make the coating: In a medium bowl, join confectioners sugar, nutmeg and cinnamon. Blend and add 1 to 2 teaspoons cream until showering consistency.

29.Half Time Hoisin Chicken Wings

<u>Ingredients</u>

- cooking spray
- ½ cup hoisin sauce
- ⅓ cup low sodium teriyaki sauce
- ¼ cup brown sugar
- 2 cloves garlic, minced
- 1 tablespoon grated fresh ginger
- 1 tablespoon chile-garlic sauce, or to taste
- 3 pounds chicken wings, cut apart at joints, wing tips discarded

Headings

- Stage 1
- Preheat the broiler to 375 degrees F (190 degrees C).
- Stage 2
- Shower a preparing sheet with cooking splash.
- Stage 3
- Whisk together hoisin sauce, teriyaki sauce, earthy colored sugar, garlic, ginger, and bean stew garlic sauce in a bowl.
- Stage 4
- Organize chicken wing pieces on the pre-arranged preparing sheet.
- Stage 5
- Brush chicken with hoisin sauce combination.
- Stage 6
- Heat in the preheated stove until chicken wings are presently not pink in the middle, 20 to 25 minutes on each side, treating like clockwork.

30.Harvested Chicken Stew

Ingredients

- 2 cups chopped onion
- 2 cups cubed, cooked boneless chicken breast meat
- 1 cup chopped celery
- 2 cups whole peeled tomatoes, with liquid
- 2 cups sliced carrots
- 5 cups chicken broth
- 1 cup sweet corn
- 1 cup peas
- 1 cup sliced zucchini

Bearings

- Stage 1
- In a huge soup pot consolidate the onion, chicken, celery, tomatoes with fluid, carrots,

stock, corn, peas and zucchini. Mix together and stew over medium low warmth for 1/2 hour, or until vegetables are cooked and delicate.

31.Harvest Vegetable Casserole

<u>Ingredients</u>

- 1 tablespoon butter
- 1 yam, quartered and sliced
- ½ sweet onion (such as Vidalia®), sliced
- 1 zucchini, halved lengthwise and sliced
- 1 yellow squash, halved lengthwise and sliced
- ½ large red bell pepper, chopped
- ½ large green bell pepper, chopped
- 1 teaspoon dried oregano
- 1 teaspoon dried basil
- salt and ground black pepper to taste
- ¼ cup shredded sharp Cheddar cheese

- 2 tablespoons seasoned bread crumbs
- butter-flavored cooking spray

Headings

- Stage 1
- Preheat broiler to 400 degrees F (200 degrees C).
- Stage 2
- Liquefy margarine in an enormous skillet over medium warmth; cook and mix sweet potato and onion in the dissolved spread until softly seared, 5 to 10 minutes. Blend zucchini, yellow squash, red ringer pepper, green chime pepper, oregano, basil, salt, and dark pepper into the sweet potato combination; cook and mix until vegetables are warmed through and somewhat delicate, 5 to 10 minutes.
- Stage 3
- Move vegetable combination to a goulash dish; sprinkle vegetables with cheddar and bread morsels. Shower top of goulash with margarine seasoned cooking splash.
- Stage 4
- Heat in the preheated broiler until garnish is seared and cheddar is softened, around 25 minutes.

32.Harvest Patties

Ingredients

- 3 yellow potatoes, peeled and grated
- 1 large carrot, peeled and grated
- 1 parsnip, peeled and grated
- 1 ½ cups grated butternut squash
- 1 egg
- ½ cup whole wheat flour
- 1 tablespoon ground cinnamon

Headings

- Stage 1
- Preheat a broiler to 400 degrees F (200 degrees C). Set up a heating sheet with cooking shower.
- Stage 2
- Throw together the potatoes, carrot, parsnip, and squash in an enormous bowl until uniformly blended. Shifting the bowl away from you, gather every one of the vegetables in

your grasp and crush them to isolate the juice. Move the vegetables into a different bowl and blend in the cinnamon.

- Stage 3
- Following 5 minutes or thereabouts, gradually spill out the juice from the principal bowl - the lower part of the bowl ought to be covered with starch. Consolidate the starch with egg and flour, utilizing a fork to mix it together. Then, at that point, take the starch blend in your grasp and back rub it through the destroyed vegetables. Separate the blend into little balls, around 1 inch thick, and level onto the pre-arranged heating sheet.
- Stage 4
- Heat the patties in the broiler until softly sautéed around the edges, around 20 minutes; flip and prepare until brilliant brown, around 5 minutes more.

33.Bleu Harvest Soup

<u>Ingredients</u>

- 8 cubes chicken bouillon
- 12 cups water
- 2 acorn squash - peeled, seeded, and diced
- 4 large carrots, sliced
- 1 tablespoon olive oil
- 1 large onion, diced
- 2 teaspoons crushed dried rosemary
- ½ pound bacon, diced
- 2 (15 ounce) cans great Northern beans, rinsed and drained
- ¾ cup crumbled blue cheese

<u>Bearings</u>

- Stage 1

- Disintegrate bouillon 3D shapes into water in a huge pot; heat to the point of boiling. Add squash to the bubbling fluid; cook until squash is starting to mellow, 6 to 8 minutes. Mix carrots into the fluid; keep cooking until carrots are simply delicate, around 5 minutes. Eliminate from warmth and put away.
- Stage 2
- Warmth oil in a skillet over medium warmth. Cook onion with rosemary in the hot oil until clear, around 5 minutes. Mix bacon into the onion; cook and mix until the bacon is fresh, 7 to 10 minutes. Scoop bacon and onion combination straightforwardly into the pot with the squash. Mix beans through the combination. Enhancement with blue cheddar to serve.

34.Harvest Pork Stew

Ingredients

- 2 tablespoons butter or oil
- 1 ½ pounds boneless pork, cut into 1/2-inch cubes
- 2 cloves garlic, minced
- 1 medium onion, chopped
- 3 cups chicken broth
- ½ teaspoon salt
- ¼ teaspoon dried rosemary, crushed
- ¼ teaspoon rubbed sage
- 1 bay leaf
- 3 cups frozen, cubed butternut squash
- 2 MacIntosh apples, cored and cubed
- 2 large potatoes, peeled and cubed (Optional)
- 2 cups carrots, peeled and diced (Optional)

Headings

- Stage 1
- Liquefy the spread in an enormous skillet over medium-high warmth. Add the pork and cook until delicately carmelized on all sides. Mix in the garlic and onion, and keep on cooking until the onion has mellowed, and the pork is firm, and at this point not pink, around 5 minutes.
- Stage 2
- Spot the pork and onions into a huge pan. Pour in the chicken stock, and season with salt, rosemary, sage, and the inlet leaf. Heat to the point of boiling, then, at that point, decrease warmth to medium-low, cover, and stew for 20 minutes.

- Stage 3
- Mix in the butternut squash, apples, potatoes, and carrots. Get back to a stew, then, at that point, cook, uncovered until the squash and apples are delicate, around 20 minutes. Eliminate the inlet leaf and serve.

35.Apple Half Moons

Ingredients

- ⅓ cup sour cream
- 1 egg yolk, beaten
- 1 teaspoon vanilla extract
- 1 ½ cups all-purpose flour
- ¼ cup white sugar
- ¾ cup butter
- 1 tablespoon butter
- 2 apple - peeled, cored, and chopped
- ¼ cup raisins
- 1 tablespoon brown sugar

- 1 teaspoon apple pie spice

<u>Bearings</u>

- Stage 1
- Mix together to mix, acrid cream, egg yolk and vanilla concentrate. In a huge bowl mix together flour and sugar. Cut in 3/4 cup spread or margarine until like coarse pieces. Blend in harsh cream combination until very much mixed.
- Stage 2
- Gap mixture fifty-fifty and chill until simple to deal with (3 hours or something like that).
- Stage 3
- To Make Filling: In little pan, soften the 1 tablespoon margarine. Add apples, raisins, earthy colored sugar and zest and cook, blending once in a while, until apples are fork delicate. Eliminate abundance fluid and cool.
- Stage 4
- Roll each piece of mixture to around 1/8 inch thickness and cut with 2-1/2 inch round cutout. Spot adjusts 1/2 inch separated on ungreased treat sheet. Spot (scanty) teaspoon of filling on each round and crease down the middle. Seal edges with fork.
- Stage 5
- Prepare at 350 degrees F (175 degrees C) for 10-12 minutes or until light brown. Eliminate and cool. Shower with lemon sugar icing made with 1/2 cup powdered sugar, 1 teaspoon lemon juice (new), 1 tablespoon water. Blend

until of sprinkling consistency. On the off chance that excessively thick, add somewhat more water, if too flimsy, somewhat more confectioners' sugar.

36.Jenna's Harvest Soup

Ingredients

- 1 (4 ounce) package Idahoan® Roasted Garlic Flavored Mashed Potatoes, dry
- 1 (32 ounce) carton reduced sodium chicken broth
- 1 (15 ounce) can prepared mashed pumpkin
- 1 pinch curry powder, or more to taste
- 1 pinch sea salt, or more to taste
- 1 pinch ground nutmeg, or more to taste
- 1 pinch ground black pepper, or more to taste
- ½ cup heavy cream

Headings

- Stage 1
- Warmth chicken stock to a weighty stew and add dry Idahoan Roasted Garlic Mashed Potatoes, pumpkin and flavors to taste.
- Stage 2
- Stew on low until to some degree thick.
- Stage 3
- Get done with cream, heat through and serve.

37.Stacy's Half Cup Sweet Potato Casserole

<u>Ingredients</u>

- ½ cup all-purpose flour
- ½ cup packed brown sugar
- ½ cup quick cooking oats
- 1 teaspoon ground cinnamon
- ½ cup butter, softened
- 1 (40 ounce) can cut yams, drained
- ½ cup whole berry cranberry sauce, drained
- 1 cup mini marshmallows

Headings

- Stage 1
- Preheat a broiler to 350 degrees F (175 degrees C).
- Stage 2
- Blend the flour, earthy colored sugar, oats, and cinnamon together in a bowl; cut the margarine into the combination until disintegrated.
- Stage 3
- Join the sweet potatoes and cranberries in a bigger bowl. Mix 1 cup of the flour combination into the sweet potatoes and cranberries; empty the blend into the lower part of a 8-inch square preparing dish and top with the leftover flour blend.
- Stage 4
- Prepare in the preheated broiler for 25 minutes; top with the marshmallows and return to the stove until the marshmallows are carmelized, around 10 minutes more.

38.Watermelon Harvest Pie

Ingredients

- 3 cups chopped watermelon rind
- 1 ⅓ cups dried cranberries
- ¾ cup chopped walnuts
- ⅓ cup distilled white vinegar
- ½ cup white sugar
- 2 teaspoons pumpkin pie spice
- 1 teaspoon all-purpose flour
- ¼ teaspoon salt
- 1 recipe pastry for a 9 inch double crust pie
- ½ cup confectioners' sugar
- 2 teaspoons orange zest
- 1 teaspoon orange juice

Headings

- Stage 1

- Preheat broiler to 425 degrees F (220 degrees C).
- Stage 2
- Spot watermelon skin in a pan and cover with water and heat this to the point of boiling. Diminish the warmth; stew revealed for around 10 minutes or until the skin becomes delicate and clear. Eliminate from warmth and channel.
- Stage 3
- Spot cooked watermelon skin in an enormous bowl and add the cranberries, pecans and vinegar. Join the sugar, pumpkin pie zest, flour, and the salt. Add this to the skin combination and mix well.
- Stage 4
- Line a 9 inch pie plate with base baked good, trim the cake even with the edge. Add the filling. Carry out the leftover baked good and make a grid hull. Seal and woodwind edges.
- Stage 5
- Cover pie with aluminum thwart and heat at 425 degrees F (175 degrees C) for 20-25 minutes. Eliminate the foil, and heat for another 20-25 minutes or until the covering is brilliant brown.
- Stage 6
- In a little bowl, join confectioners sugar, orange skin and squeezed orange. Mix to join, and spoon over hot pie. Cool on a wire rack.

39.Harvest Pumpkin Soup

Ingredients

- 2 small sugar pumpkin
- 3 cups chicken stock
- ¾ cup heavy whipping cream
- ¼ teaspoon ground nutmeg
- ½ teaspoon ground sage
- 1 ½ teaspoons salt
- 4 tablespoons sour cream

Headings

- Stage 1
- Preheat broiler to 400 degrees F (205 degrees C). Slice pumpkins down the middle and scoop out seeds. Shower a treat sheet with non-stick cooking splash. Spot pumpkins, tissue side down on the treat sheet and meal until delicate to the touch, around 45 minutes. Eliminate

pumpkins from broiler and let cool. When pumpkins are cool scratch tissue from skins into a food processor. Dispose of skins.

- Stage 2
- Add chicken stock to the pumpkin and puree. Empty soup into an enormous pan and bring to a stew over medium warmth. Mix in cream, nutmeg, savvy and salt. Blend well and eliminate from heat. Serve embellished with a touch of acrid cream

40.Harvest Vegan Nut Roast

Ingredients

- ½ cup chopped celery
- 2 onions, chopped
- ¾ cup walnuts
- ¾ cup pecan or sunflower meal
- 2 ½ cups soy milk

- 1 teaspoon dried basil
- 1 teaspoon dried oregano
- 3 cups bread crumbs
- salt and pepper to taste

Bearings

- Stage 1
- Preheat stove to 350 degrees F (175 degrees C). Daintily oil a portion skillet.
- Stage 2
- In a medium size skillet, saute the slashed celery and the onion in 3 teaspoons water until cooked.
- Stage 3
- In a huge blending bowl join the celery and onion with pecans, walnut or sunflower dinner, soy milk, basil, oregano, bread morsels, salt and pepper to taste; blend well. Spot combination in the pre-arranged portion container.
- Stage 4
- Prepare for 60 to an hour and a half; until the portion is cooked through.

41.Da Beef Lover's Half Time Stuffed Meatloaf

<u>Ingredients</u>

- 1 cup instant rice
- 2 pounds ground beef sirloin
- 1 pound ground beef round
- 1 egg
- 1 onion, chopped
- 1 large green bell pepper, seeded and chopped
- 1 (4 ounce) can mushrooms, drained
- garlic powder to taste
- salt and ground black pepper to taste
- 1 cup grated Parmesan cheese
- 1 (12 fluid ounce) can spinach, drained
- ¼ pound thinly sliced deli ham
- ¼ pound thinly sliced salami
- ¼ pound thinly sliced Swiss cheese

<u>Bearings</u>

- Stage 1
- Preheat stove to 375 degrees F (190 degrees C). Delicately oil a shallow broiling dish. Get ready moment rice as per bundle bearings.
- Stage 2
- In a huge bowl, combine as one ground sirloin, ground round, egg, hacked onion, green pepper, mushrooms and cooked rice. Season with garlic powder, salt and pepper.
- Stage 3
- On clean ledge, orchestrate sheets of wax paper roughly 1/2 feet in length by 1 foot wide. Spot meat combination on wax paper, and straighten into an enormous square, around 1/2 inch thick (the more slender the better). Sprinkle with more garlic powder, then, at that point, layer with parmesan, spinach, ham, salami and Swiss cheddar. Utilizing the wax paper, roll the meat as firmly as could really be expected while eliminating the wax paper as you go. Get the two open finishes into the actual meatloaf, and with hands gently covered in vegetable oil, shape into a portion. While lifting with the wax paper, move to shallow simmering container, then, at that point, slide wax paper out from under.
- Stage 4
- Prepare in preheated stove for 1 hour and 10 minutes, or until meat is as of now not pink and squeezes run clear. Permit to cool 15 minutes prior to serving.

42.Half-hour Pudding Cake (Montreal Pudding)

Ingredients

- 1 cup all-purpose flour
- ⅓ cup white sugar
- 1 teaspoon baking powder
- ½ cup raisins
- ½ cup milk
- 1 cup packed brown sugar
- 2 cups boiling water
- 1 tablespoon butter
- 1 teaspoon vanilla extract

Bearings

- Stage 1
- Preheat stove to 350 degrees F (175 degrees C). Spread one 2 quart goulash dish.

- Stage 2
- Filter the flour, white sugar and preparing powder together. Add the raisins and mix in the milk. Spoon hitter into the pre-arranged dish.
- Stage 3
- Consolidate the earthy colored sugar, bubbling water, margarine and vanilla. Tenderly pour over the player. Try not to mix.
- Stage 4
- Prepare at 350 degrees F (175 degrees C) for 30 minutes. Serve warm.

43.November Harvest Casserole

<u>Ingredients</u>

- 1 butternut squash, halved and seeded

- 2 sweet potatoes, halved lengthwise
- 2 ¾ cups water
- ¼ teaspoon salt
- 1 ½ cups whole grain couscous
- 5 links precooked apple chicken sausage, sliced into rounds
- 1 green bell pepper, diced
- ½ cup diced green onion
- 1 (12 ounce) package shredded mozzarella cheese

Bearings

- Stage 1
- Preheat stove to 350 degrees F (175 degrees C). Spot butternut squash and yams cut-side down on the preparing sheet.
- Stage 2
- Prepare in the preheated broiler until relaxed, around 30 minutes. Cool until effectively dealt with, 5 to 10 minutes. Scoop sort through of the skins; place in a 9x13-inch goulash dish.
- Stage 3
- Heat water and salt to the point of boiling in a little pot. Mix in couscous; stew over medium-high warmth until couscous is delicate, around 5 minutes. Channel abundance water.
- Stage 4
- Mix couscous, wiener, green ringer pepper, and green onion into the goulash dish. Sprinkle mozzarella cheddar on top. Cover meal dish firmly with aluminum foil.
- Stage 5

- Prepare in the preheated broiler until hot and effervescent, 30 to 40 minutes.

44.Chicken Half Moons

Ingredients

- 1 skinless, boneless chicken breast half
- 1 onion, chopped
- ½ cup cubed Cheddar cheese
- 2 ½ cups all-purpose flour
- 3 eggs
- 1 cup water
- 1 egg
- 1 tablespoon water

Headings

- Stage 1
- Softly oil an enormous skillet and cook chicken until as of now not pink; eliminate and hold.
- Stage 2

- In a food processor, add onion to puree, then, at that point, add cheddar to puree. Add chicken and puree a last time.
- Stage 3
- In an enormous bowl, add flour and make a well in the middle. Add eggs and blend well; add water and change with flour and water depending on the situation. Mixture ought to be versatile, yet not tacky.
- Stage 4
- In a little bowl, beat 1 egg and add one tablespoon of water. On a floured surface, carry out mixture until it is 1/4 inch thick or nearly paper meager. Remove 2 inch circles and brush with egg and water combination. Spot 1 teaspoon of stuffing in the circle and overlap over. Seal the half moon by creasing the edge.
- Stage 5
- Heat an enormous pot of softly salted water to the point of boiling. Add half moons and cook for 2 to 3 minutes or until still somewhat firm; channel and serve.

45.Apple Harvest Pound Cake with Caramel Glaze

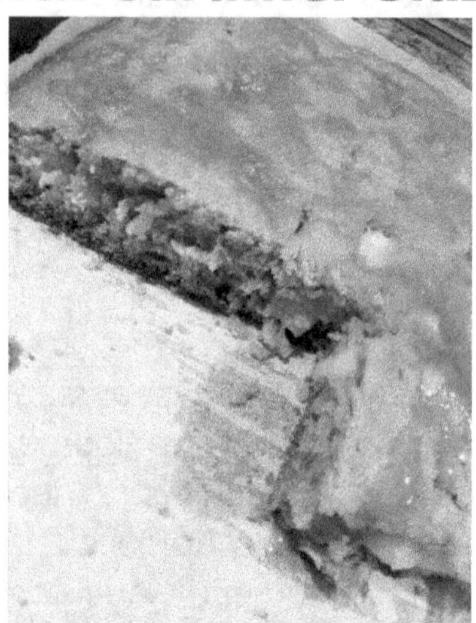

Ingredients

- 2 cups white sugar
- 1 ½ cups vegetable oil
- 2 teaspoons vanilla extract
- 3 eggs
- 3 cups all-purpose flour
- 1 teaspoon baking soda
- ½ teaspoon ground cinnamon
- 1 teaspoon salt
- 2 medium Granny Smith apples - peeled, cored and chopped
- 1 cup chopped walnuts
- ½ cup butter or margarine
- 2 teaspoons milk
- ½ cup brown sugar

Headings

- Stage 1
- Preheat the broiler to 350 degrees F (175 degrees C). Oil a 9 inch Bundt container.
- Stage 2
- In an enormous bowl, beat the sugar, oil, vanilla and eggs with an electric blender until light and feathery. Consolidate the flour, preparing pop, cinnamon and salt; mix into the player just until mixed. Overlap in the apples and pecans utilizing a spoon. Fill the pre-arranged skillet.
- Stage 3
- Heat for 1 hour and 20 minutes in the preheated broiler, until a toothpick embedded into the crown or the cake tells the truth. Permit to cool for around 20 minutes then, at that point, modify on to a wire rack.
- Stage 4
- Make the coating by warming the spread, milk and earthy colored sugar in a little pot over medium warmth. Heat to the point of boiling, mixing to break up the sugar, then, at that point, eliminate from the warmth. Shower over the warm cake. I like to put a sheet of aluminum foil under the cooling rack to get the dribbles for simple tidy up.

46.Harvest Breakfast Pitas

Ingredients

- 1 cup peeled, seeded, and cubed butternut squash
- 1 cup peeled and cubed sweet potatoes
- 1 tablespoon olive oil
- 1 teaspoon salt
- 1 teaspoon ground black pepper
- 2 links apple chicken sausage (such as Aidells®), thinly sliced and quartered
- 4 eggs
- 2 cups fresh baby spinach
- 1 tablespoon red pepper flakes, or to taste
- 1 cup canned black beans, rinsed and drained
- 2 tablespoons goat cheese, or to taste
- 2 large whole-wheat pita breads, toasted and halved

Headings

- Stage 1
- Preheat broiler to 375 degrees F (190 degrees C).
- Stage 2
- Join butternut squash, yams, olive oil, salt, and pepper in a capacity compartment. Cover with top and shake well until completely covered. Spot vegetables onto a heating sheet.
- Stage 3
- Heat in the preheated stove until vegetables are handily penetrated with a fork, around 45 minutes.
- Stage 4
- Spot chicken frankfurter in a huge skillet and cook over medium-high warmth, turning once in a while, until equitably seared, around 10 minutes. Lessen warmth to medium-low; add eggs, spinach, and red pepper chips. Cook and mix until eggs are set, around 5 minutes. Blend in dark beans; cook until warmed through, around 1 moment. Add goat cheddar.
- Stage 5
- Fill pita breads with fried eggs and heated vegetables.

47.Harvest Salad from Oikos

Ingredients

- 1 cup Dannon Oikos Plain Greek Nonfat Yogurt
- 2 ounces crumbled goat cheese
- 2 tablespoons cider vinegar
- 2 tablespoons chopped parsley
- Salt and cracked pepper
- 3 heads crisp Romaine hearts, shredded
- 1 large apple, cored and sliced
- 8 ounces roasted turkey, julienned
- ½ cup dried cranberries
- ½ cup toasted pecans

Bearings

- Stage 1

- In a bowl combine as one, yogurt, goat cheddar, vinegar, parsley, salt and broke pepper. Let stand 15 minutes.
- Stage 2
- In a huge bowl join remaining fixings. Throw dressing with greens and throw tenderly to cover. Separation salad equitably among 6 plates (2 cups for each).

48.Summer Pasta with Basil, Tomatoes and Cheese

Ingredients

- 2 pounds vine ripened tomatoes, seeded and diced
- 3 cloves garlic, minced
- ½ cup chopped fresh basil
- 1 tablespoon chopped fresh mint leaves
- ¾ teaspoon salt
- ½ teaspoon freshly ground black pepper
- ¼ teaspoon crushed red pepper flakes

* ½ cup olive oil
* ¼ cup cream sherry
* 12 ounces spaghetti
* ½ cup freshly grated Asiago cheese
* 2 cups fontina cheese, shredded

<u>Bearings</u>

* Stage 1
* In a medium bowl, throw together tomatoes, garlic, basil, mint, salt and dark pepper, hot pepper chips, olive oil, and cream sherry. Let remain at room temperature for as long as 2 hours, mixing every so often.
* Stage 2
* Cook the pasta In an enormous pot of bubbling salted water until delicate, yet firm to the nibble.
* Stage 3
* Channel the pasta, and move to an enormous serving bowl. Channel 1/4 cup of the fluid from the tomato combination, and throw with the pasta to cover. Add cheddar, and throw until it starts to soften. Add the tomato combination, and throw until blended.

49.Mussels Pasta

Ingredients

- 3 tablespoons olive oil, divided
- ¼ onion, chopped
- 1 clove garlic, minced
- 1 cup tomato sauce
- salt and ground black pepper to taste
- 1 clove garlic, peeled
- 25 mussels, cleaned and debearded
- 1 splash dry white wine
- 20 clams in shell, scrubbed
- ½ teaspoon red pepper flakes, or to taste
- 2 tablespoons chopped fresh parsley, or to taste
- 4 tablespoons freshly grated Parmesan cheese, or to taste

Headings

- Stage 1
- Warmth 1 tablespoon olive oil in a pan over medium warmth and cook onion until delicate and clear, 3 to 5 minutes. Add minced garlic and cook until fragrant, around 30 seconds. Add pureed tomatoes, season with salt, and stew over low warmth until thickened, around 15 minutes.
- Stage 2
- Warmth 1 tablespoon olive oil in a skillet and cook stripped garlic for 1 moment. Add mussels and cook until they open, around 8 minutes. Move mussels to a bowl. Pour in white wine and permit to vanish. Eliminate garlic, yet save cooking fluid.
- Stage 3
- Warmth 1 tablespoon olive oil in a different skillet and cook shellfishes until they open, around 8 minutes. Eliminate 1/2 of the mussels and 1/2 of the shellfishes from their shells. Dispose of any unopened shells. Add all mussels and shellfishes, with and without shells, and cooking fluid to the pureed tomatoes. Season with red pepper drops and stew for a couple of moments.
- Stage 4
- In the mean time, heat an enormous pot of daintily salted water to the point of boiling. Cook spaghetti in the bubbling water, blending once in a while, until delicate yet firm to the chomp, around 12 minutes. Channel and add spaghetti to pureed tomatoes. Blend in parsley

and season with salt and pepper. Present with Parmesan as an afterthought.

50.Chop Chop Salad

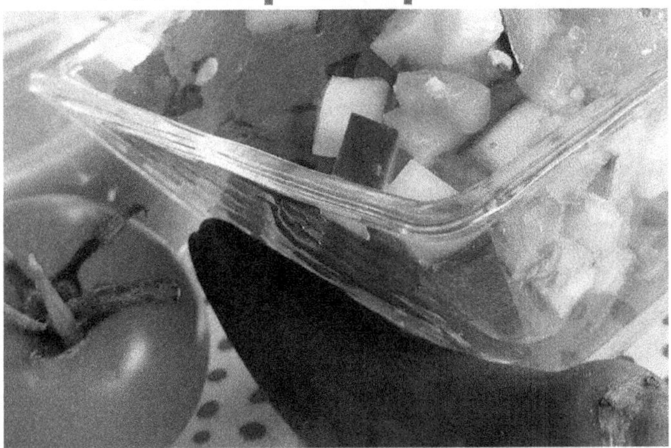

Ingredients

- 1 red grapefruit
- 1 cup peeled, chopped jicama
- 1 cup chopped orange bell pepper
- 1 cup chopped cucumber
- 1 tomato, chopped
- 2 green onions, chopped
- ¼ cup chopped fresh cilantro

Headings

- Stage 1
- With an extremely sharp blade, cut a cut from the base and top of the grapefruit, cutting into the natural product. Stand the grapefruit up on a work surface, and cut off the strip and white essence in vertical cuts, uncovering the natural

product portions (cut marginally into the natural product part). Utilize your blade to tenderly cut between the uncovered white films, and extricate the grapefruit portions into a bowl. Choose any seeds.

- Stage 2
- Spot the grapefruit areas, jicama, orange ringer pepper, cucumber, tomato, green onions, and cilantro into a serving of mixed greens bowl, and throw tenderly to blend.

51.Baked Brie

Ingredients

- 6 slices sun-dried tomatoes in oil, minced
- 3 artichoke hearts packed in oil, drained and chopped
- 2 cloves garlic, minced
- 1 (1 1/2 pound) Brie cheese round

Bearings

- Stage 1
- Preheat stove to 370 degrees F (187 degrees C).
- Stage 2
- Blend sun-dried tomatoes, artichoke hearts, and garlic in a little bowl.
- Stage 3
- Trim the top piece of the skin from the Brie round and dispose of. Spot Brie round in a gather heating dish with the managed side confronting together; top with the tomato combination.
- Stage 4
- Prepare in preheated broiler until cheddar is relaxed, around 20 minutes.

52.Sausage Bake

Ingredients

- 1 ½ pounds bulk pork sausage
- 3 ½ cups milk, divided
- 8 eggs
- ¾ teaspoon dry mustard
- 8 slices bread, torn into small squares
- 2 cups shredded mozzarella cheese
- 1 (10.75 ounce) can condensed cream of mushroom soup

Headings

- Stage 1
- Warmth an enormous skillet over medium-high warmth. Cook and mix frankfurter in the hot skillet until carmelized and brittle, 5 to 7 minutes; channel and dispose of oil.
- Stage 2
- Beat 2 1/2 cups milk, eggs, and mustard in an enormous bowl.
- Stage 3
- Spread bread squares into the lower part of a heating dish. Layer mozzarella cheddar on the bread and top with frankfurter. Pour the egg combination over the whole dish. Cover the heating dish with saran wrap and refrigerate 8 hours to expedite.
- Stage 4
- Preheat broiler to 300 degrees F (150 degrees C).
- Stage 5

- Mix cream of mushroom soup and 1 cup milk together in a bowl. Eliminate and dispose of saran wrap from heating dish. Pour soup combination over the 'heat.'
- Stage 6
- Heat in preheated broiler until hot in the middle, around an hour and a half.

53.Baked Apricots

Ingredients

- 3 (15 ounce) cans apricot halves, drained
- ¾ cup packed brown sugar
- 50 buttery round crackers, crumbled
- ½ cup butter, melted

Headings

- Stage 1

- Preheat broiler to 325 degrees F (165 degrees C).
- Stage 2
- In a 8x12 inch heating container, layer half of apricots, earthy colored sugar, saltine morsels, and margarine. Rehash.
- Stage 3
- Heat for 50 to an hour.

54.Baked Pompano

<u>Ingredients</u>

- 1 cup soy sauce
- ½ cup rice cooking wine
- 5 tablespoons olive oil, divided
- 2 teaspoons hoisin sauce
- 2 teaspoons fish sauce
- 2 teaspoons oyster sauce

- 1 lime, halved
- 1 shallot, diced
- 1 (2 inch) piece peeled fresh ginger, diced
- 1 (1 1/2) pound whole pompano fish, gutted and cleaned
- 1 teaspoon dried dill, or to taste
- salt and ground black pepper to taste
- 2 cups napa cabbage leaves, or as needed

Headings

- Stage 1
- Whisk soy sauce, rice wine, 1 tablespoon olive oil, hoisin sauce, fish sauce, clam sauce, and squeeze of 1/2 the lime together in a bowl.
- Stage 2
- Warmth 3 tablespoons olive oil in a skillet over medium warmth. Cook and mix shallot and ginger until beginning to brown, around 2 minutes. Pour in soy sauce combination; stew until marginally thickened, 5 to 10 minutes.
- Stage 3
- Score the two sides of the pompano in a crosshatch design. Wipe off with a paper towel. Season the two sides and within the pompano with dill, salt, and pepper. Cut leftover 1/2 of the lime and orchestrate cuts inside. Shower staying 1 tablespoon olive oil over pompano; rub over the two sides.
- Stage 4
- Layer cabbage leaves in the lower part of an enormous preparing dish; place pompano on top. Pour soy sauce combination over

pompano. Cover heating dish with aluminum foil. Let marinate as broiler preheats.

- Stage 5
- Preheat stove to 400 degrees F (200 degrees C).
- Stage 6
- Prepare pompano in the preheated stove until fragrant, around 20 minutes. Eliminate aluminum foil; keep preparing until pompano chips effectively with a fork, around 10 minutes more.
- Stage 7
- Strip back skin and lift pompano tissue off the bones utilizing a fork. Move to a serving plate.

55.Baked Pancakes

<u>Ingredients</u>

- 3 tablespoons butter
- ½ cup all-purpose flour
- ½ cup milk
- 2 eggs, beaten
- 1 teaspoon white sugar
- ¼ teaspoon salt
- ¼ lemon, juiced (Optional)
- 1 tablespoon confectioners' sugar, or to taste (Optional)

Headings

- Stage 1
- Preheat broiler to 425 degrees F (220 degrees C).
- Stage 2
- Put margarine in a 9-inch pie skillet. Spot container in the preheating broiler until margarine is dissolved, 5 to 10 minutes.
- Stage 3
- Whisk flour, milk, eggs, white sugar, and salt together in a bowl; empty blend into the hot spread.
- Stage 4
- Prepare in the preheated stove until flapjack is brown on the edges and a toothpick embedded in the middle tells the truth, 20 to 24 minutes. Press lemon over flapjack and sprinkle with confectioners' sugar.

56.Baked Eggplant

<u>Ingredients</u>

- cooking spray
- 1 eggplant, sliced into 1/2-inch-thick rounds
- 3 tomatoes, sliced
- 1 tablespoon extra virgin olive oil
- 1 teaspoon oregano
- ⅓ cup grated Parmesan cheese
- salt and ground black pepper to taste

<u>Bearings</u>

- Stage 1
- Preheat stove to 400 degrees F (200 degrees C). Set up a preparing dish with non-stick play.
- Stage 2
- Orchestrate eggplant and tomato cuts into the lower part of the pre-arranged preparing dish. Shower olive oil over the vegetables; season

with oregano, salt, and pepper. Sprinkle Parmesan cheddar over the whole blend.

- Stage 3
- Prepare in preheated stove until the cheddar is starting to brown, around 30 minutes. Change stove oven to high; keep preparing until totally seared, around 5 minutes.

57.No Bake Bars

Ingredients

- 1 cup Karo Light Corn Syrup
- 1 cup sugar
- 1 cup creamy peanut butter
- 6 cups crispy rice cereal
- 1 cup semi-sweet chocolate chips
- 1 cup butterscotch chips

Bearings

- Stage 1
- Cook corn syrup and sugar together in a huge dish over medium warmth, blending to disintegrate sugar. Heat blend to the point of boiling. Eliminate from heat. Mix in peanut butter; blend well. Add cereal; mix until equitably covered.
- Stage 2
- Fill lubed 13x9-inch container and pat into the right spot.
- Stage 3
- Liquefy chocolate and butterscotch chips together in pot over low warmth, blending continually. Spread over oat.
- Stage 4
- Cool something like 45 minutes, or until firm. Cut into bars.

58.Baked Penne

Ingredients

- ½ pound extra lean ground beef
- ½ cup chopped onions
- ½ cup chopped green peppers
- 1 (24 ounce) jar spaghetti sauce
- 1 (10 ounce) tub PHILADELPHIA Italian Cheese and Herb Cooking Creme, divided
- 1 cup KRAFT Shredded Mozzarella Cheese, divided
- 3 cups hot cooked penne pasta

Bearings

- Stage 1
- Warmth stove to 350 degrees F.
- Stage 2

- Earthy colored meat with vegetables in huge nonstick skillet. Mix in spaghetti sauce, 3/4 cup cooking creme and 1/2 cup mozzarella: cook and mix 2 to 3 min. or on the other hand until mozzarella is liquefied. Add pasta; blend daintily.
- Stage 3
- Spoon into 2-qt. meal; top with residual cooking creme and mozzarella. Cover.
- Stage 4
- Prepare 20 min. or on the other hand until warmed through, revealing after 15 min.

59.Baked Corn

Ingredients

- 1 (15.25 ounce) can whole kernel corn
- 1 (14.75 ounce) can cream-style corn
- ½ cup sour cream

- 1 cup butter or margarine, melted
- 2 eggs
- 1 (12 ounce) package corn muffin mix

Headings

- Stage 1
- Preheat broiler to 350 degrees F (175 degrees C).
- Stage 2
- Join the entire piece corn, cream-style corn, sharp cream, liquefied spread or margarine, beaten eggs and corn biscuit blend. Blend well and fill one 9x13 inch heating dish.
- Stage 3
- Heat at 350 degrees F (175 degrees C) for 35 to 45 minutes.

60.Baked Potato

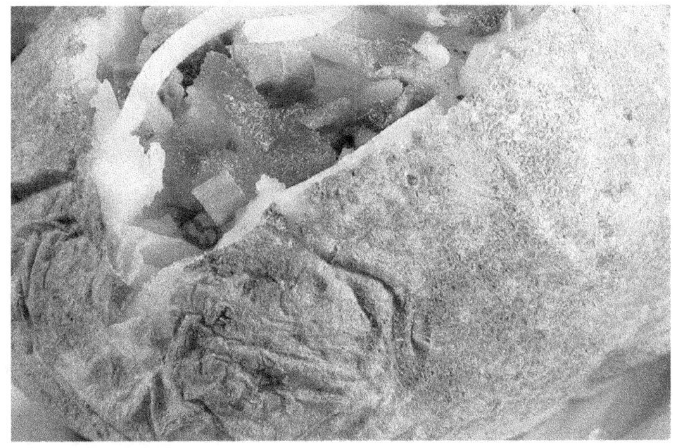

Ingredients

- 1 baking potato

Bearings

- Stage 1
- Preheat stove to 350 degrees F (175 degrees C).
- Stage 2
- Scour the potato and prick it with a fork to keep steam from developing and making the potato detonate in your stove.
- Stage 3
- Prepare for 1/2 hours.

61.Baked Omelet

Ingredients

- 8 eggs
- 1 cup milk
- ½ teaspoon seasoning salt
- 3 ounces cooked ham, diced
- ½ cup shredded Cheddar cheese
- ½ cup shredded mozzarella cheese
- 1 tablespoon dried minced onion

Headings

- Stage 1
- Preheat broiler to 350 degrees F (175 degrees C). Oil one 8x8 inch goulash dish and put away.
- Stage 2
- Beat together the eggs and milk. Add preparing salt, ham, cheddar, Mozzarella cheddar and minced onion. Fill arranged goulash dish.
- Stage 3
- Heat uncovered at 350 degrees F (175 degrees C) for 40 to 45 minutes.

62.Baked Peaches

Ingredients

- 1 (16 ounce) package frozen peach slices
- ⅓ cup brown sugar substitute

- ¼ cup pecans
- 1 tablespoon all-purpose flour
- 1 teaspoon vanilla extract

<u>Bearings</u>

- Stage 1
- Preheat stove to 350 degrees F (175 degrees C).
- Stage 2
- Spread peach cuts into a preparing dish in a solitary layer. Mix earthy colored sugar substitute, walnuts, flour, and vanilla concentrate together; spread over the peach cuts.
- Stage 3
- Prepare in preheated stove until the peaches are warmed through, 20 to 30 minutes.